SYRIAN EXPLORATION.

American Geographical and Statistical Society.

REPORT AND MEMORIAL

ON

SYRIAN EXPLORATION

SOCIETY'S ROOMS:
N. Y. UNIVERSITY, WASHINGTON SQUARE,
NEW YORK.
1857.

REPORT.

To the Committee on Syrian Exploration of the American Geographical and Statistical Society:

THIS report is respectfully submitted by the Chairman of the Committee as explanatory of the annexed memorial, and the commercial importance of Syrian Arabia.

An eminent statesman, the Hon. Robert J. Walker, in a recent publication, says, "It is now more than twenty years since, in the Senate of the United States, when the bill was pending to distribute among the States, under the fiction of a deposit never to be recalled, the surplus revenue of thirty-eight millions of dollars, I suggested the application of that fund to the purchase of California and New Mexico to the line of 32, with a quit-claim to Texas, with the consent of that republic. Had this proposition then succeeded, all that vast territory would then have been ours. It would have saved the war with Mexico, at an expense of so many thousand precious lives, of nearly one hundred millions of treasure, of fifteen millions in addition for California, and ten millions besides for the Gadsen purchase. Among the reasons then given by me for that measure was this, that upon observing the map of our continent, the course of the Red River and the Gila, the break in the Rocky Mountains, by the Rio del Norte, at El Paso, and of the Sierra Madre, by the Gila River, nature seemed to indicate the proper railroad route to the Pacific. I have often reflected what great results, so favorable to our country, would have followed the success at that time of that proposition.

The railroad to San Francisco would long since have been completed, the gold discoveries of California would have been made in 1836, the gold of that region, as well as of Australia, and the gold and silver of the Gila region, poured into our country; and already *the command of the commerce of the world* would have been seen passing from England to America —from London to New York. The records of the State department and dispatches will show that the eminent statesman just elected to the Chief Magistracy of the Union, participated in these views."

In a late number of a foreign journal, "The Nautical Magazine," it is stated, "Of the two projected canals, that of America and that of Suez, the importance is very different. The canal of Suez would unite India and Europe. It would re-establish the commerce and prosperity, the peace and advancement, of Europe, Asia, and even Africa; in a word, of the whole of this hemisphere, the continental superficies of which, compared with that of the opposite, being in the proportion of 23 to 11."

"The command of the commerce of the world," or "the advancement of the eastern hemisphere" alone, are not now of so much importance as the increase of trade among all people and on both hemispheres. The want of employment is at least felt by the benevolent. The great geographical error of the day seems to be that of regarding the world as a formation of halves. The exploration of unknown regions, and the application of all as well as the best modes of transit, are wanted to develop the resources of every country. Petty national jealousies will in this way be removed, and the arts of peace take the place of those of war.

The many scientific expeditions of late years lead us to hope, that we are rapidly approaching a period when but little will be left to discover. The late Japan and Arctic expeditions, those of South America, the North Pacific, Africa, and the islands of the ocean, by governments of both hemispheres, prove that our expectations are well founded. In this matter of exploration and scientific research, we would have all nations to vie with each other. The present Pasha of Egypt has already made extensive surveys, at much expense, for the great Isthmus of Suez Canal. The scientific expedition to the sources of the Nile, and the subject of growing cotton in the district watered by the river Tigris, are equally engaging his attention. This seems to be an example worthy of the intelligent consideration of other powers.

The future greatness of this western hemisphere is most probably to be shown in *her commerce of the seas.* The wealth, population and increasing trade of the eastern hemisphere, render it comparatively better adapted than the western for a continuous line of railroad. All countries are particularly interested in every isthmus. To convince ourselves of these facts we have but to study the map of the world—to look at what is doing in both hemispheres, in steamships, projected railroads and telegraphs—to glance at the comparative amount of land and water between two distant points, such as London and Sidney. It is for the interest, therefore, of every individual to push forward this age of commerce and civilization, remembering that the greatest attainable speed is of inconceivable importance. Like other nations with reference to our continent, we, as Americans, are attracted to the country lying between the Mediterranean Sea and the Persian Gulf. This, also, like more than one isthmus, divides the waters of the Atlantic and the Pacific. Railroads and telegraphs are now proposed in this neighborhood, to connect Europe and Asia, England and New Holland, London, Bombay and Sidney. It will soon be a matter of history, that vessels formerly left Europe, or the Atlantic ports of North America, to steer for the Canaries or Azores, in order to find the trade winds of the northern hemisphere, to make the coast of Brazil, and sight Cape Frio, or put into the harbor of Rio Janeiro, to double the Cape of Good Hope, *en route* for India and China.

The interest which at least every maritime nation should take in an isthmus, is a subject in itself. The isthmus sections, or, as they may be called in two instances, the enlarged isthmus, is seen in both hemispheres. Syrian Arabia, including Palestine, to the Isthmus of Suez, is the enlarged isthmus of the eastern hemisphere. This section has now some striking resemblances to Central America, of the western hemisphere. The political and commercial importance of both is well understood in Europe generally, especially in the two proposed ship-canals of the Isthmus of Suez and Darien, besides the various projected railways. Many here watch the movements in the East; and all are familiar with the expedition sent out three years ago by the governments of England, France and the United States, to survey the Isthmus of Darien. It would be gratifying if Syrian Arabia could be explored in a similar manner.

We quote what has been said of Central America, for the sake of comparison.

"It has a situation unsurpassed by any portion of the world, not excepting Great Britain, for commercial purposes. Forming, by a narrow isthmus, a separation between the great seas which constitute the field of navigation, and comprising the theatre of foreign commerce for the globe, and being very nearly central in latitude between the poles, *it is, in fact, commercially the centre of our world.* There are, at this time, but two routes of transit,—one at the Bay of Panama, in the extreme south beyond the territory of the United States, by railroad; and one across Nicaragua, by river and lake. Two others are about to be constructed, viz., one in Honduras, consisting of a railroad extending from Puerto de Caballos, on the Atlantic coast, to San Lorenzo or Amapalla, on the Pacific, in the Bay of Fonseca, distance 160 miles, which, we understand, is to be commenced the ensuing spring; the other at the Isthmus of Tehuantepec, in Mexico, which is already in progress. Both of these new routes will probably be open for passengers and freight within two years. That which is the third named, has, in the opinion of Mr. Squier, advantages over all others. It has excellent ports at each end of the route."

Besides, we have the new project for cutting a ship-canal across the Isthmus of Darien, from Caledonia Bay on the Atlantic side to the Gulf of San Miguel on the Pacific. The "London Times" devotes a leading article to this project, and invites public attention to the matter of an interoceanic ship canal, as a work affecting the interests of mankind, and of vast importance on every ground, political, social, and commercial. The same journal recommends the proposition to public discussion and minute investigation, with a view to elicit more full and accurate information as to the feasibility of this, or any similar enterprise. As late as Dec. 10th, 1856, it remarks :

> "Of what incalculable service to mankind would it have been, had a few millions been devoted to effecting a passage through the American Isthmus. This we have not done, while we have wasted hundreds of millions upon powder and ball, gunships and shells. We care not at what point of the American Isthmus, between the mouth of the San Juan, which communicates with the Nicaragua Lake, to that of the Atrato, which falls into the Gulf of Darien, the ground be broken, but at some point or another, unless the English, American, and French engineers acknowledge themselves vanquished, it should be done. We are not desirous to see the canal exclusively in the hands of British monopolists. The work affects the common interests of mankind ; and the more numerous the nations which are concerned in it, the fewer are the chances that the free passage will be interrupted by the contingencies of future warfare.
>
> "The population of the whole territory of Central America is at present only about 2,000,000. Its capacity with a population about as dense as Massachusetts, would be about or nearly 20,000,0 C0 ; or as dense as Belgium, not far from 50,000,000.
>
> "In addition to the advantage of commercial situation, Central America has, for the most part, a salubrious climate, and a soil of exuberant fertility, producing all tropical fruits in excess, and a crop of Indian corn every three months throughout the year."

We have but to look at the vast regions and populations of Asia, to know that the trade of the East is but in its infancy. Jewish influence brought to bear, by a proper representation, in what is called Syrian Arabia, would most effectually give a new impetus to the commerce of the East, as well as of the world. The best representative of all nations is the Jewish. Their commercial taste and interests are such as to unite them on some central commercial mart, provided they are protected. Their influence is well seen in New York, the great commercial metropolis of the United States, where they already nearly outnumber their brethren of the whole United Kingdom of Great Britain and Ireland. The anticipated effects on all countries of this daily increasing influence in New York, is not a matter of little moment. It is seen in the twenty-two synagogues of this city, known not so much by their names, as by their various national distinctions. The indifference or neglect of the religious association of "The Holy Land" by the Western

Jew, is more than made up by the zeal of those of the East. But while congregating in such large numbers in the New World, they are still largely represented in many parts of the Old. A recent writer states, among other facts concerning the Jews in Abyssinia, China, and Hindostan, that "the Hindoo-Chinese Israelites in the single city of Bombay number 5000." It would appear that Jews were always numerous in Arabia, the population of which is estimated at 12,000,000. Jewish observances are said to characterize many tribes in Southern Arabia professing Islam. Some are to be found in all the chief market-towns of Arabia, except in the Hejaz, where they are forbidden. In Yemen, the native Jews still form a considerable community ; and further north, towards Syria, are the warlike tribes of the Beni Hobáb, who cloak Jewish faith under a Mahometan exterior. Among them are the Beni Arhab (Rechab), who, proud of their descent, assume the title of "The Sword of Yemen." On the south coast of Arabia, the natives manifest very generally a striking indifference to the precepts of the Koran. There is the influence of the Jews, as connected with the commerce of the interior of Africa, and the caravan trade to Mecca. In no place on the Mediterranean Sea is their wealth greater and more used for trade than in Northern Africa. The Jews of Barbary are governed by their own laws. Their number is estimated at 700,000. They are stated to be the only working class, and are all a very laborious people. In Tunis they are in possession of many monopolies, and some of them are enormously rich. Here they are the best mechanics. The keeping of the jewels and valuables of the Bey is entrusted to them, and they are thus his treasurers, private secretaries, and interpreters. The little that is known of medicine, science, and art, is for the most part confined to them. Those in Tunis have a kaid, or governor, appointed by the Bey, and who may be considered as their first magistrate in all things temporal ; but their spiritual concerns are managed by their chief rabbi, who possesses great power, more than even the kaid himself. In Algiers, the upper classes of the Jews transact business with the European merchants ; those of the middle and lower classes act as agents to the

Arabs and Berbers. At Algiers, an Arab would not sell a couple of fowls without the aid of a Jew.

"The Jews have, by foreign and home trade, rendered essential service to Europe. Their enterprise has stimulated that of the Christians, and opened the way to modern trade! In England, as well as in France, in Germany as well as in Holland, they can now point with just pride to their own people, eminent in banking, in commerce, science, letters, and arts. The house of Rothschild has made contracts with the principal sovereigns of Europe; and the Pope himself, finding his coffers empty, has stooped to ask favors of a Jew."

It should be remembered, that under Charlemagne and his successors, the Jews were the merchants of all France; and that there also they seconded the Protestants in their noble opposition to the oppressors of the truth in the struggles for religious liberty.

The Arabs may be all divided into three classes—the inhabitants of towns, the cultivators of the soil, and the Bedouin, or people of the wilderness. In the flourishing days of the Caliphs, the Arab merchant visited China, the interior of Africa, the shores of the Baltic, and Siberia. In truth, Arab commerce embraced, at one time, nearly the whole world as then known.

A colonization, in which all are represented, is for the interest of trade. This is the germ of a true "balance of power," as it is unfriendly to no one nation. This "Congress of Nations," necessarily and by association interested in all mankind, would give to the future of Syrian Arabia "the command of the commerce of the world." To prove the central position of Syrian Arabia, we have to remember its peculiar position in the greatest of the two hemispheres. The desert which lies between the rivers Jordan and Euphrates, as has been well said, "was made by man, not by God," and is only such during the dry season. The planting of trees will, as is well known, remedy this evil.

Although we have but little knowledge of the botany of this region, and more especially of the trees, yet the cultivation of the olive is known to be very profitable. Our intelligent representative in Syria and Palestine has recently made the introduction of this tree into the United States, and that only on account of its profit, the subject of one of his interesting letters from the East. He says, "The people here call the olive plantation the 'Mother of Widows and Orphans,' and 'the Widow's Property,' because the product is so large, and so little care and labor are required in managing the plantation. Even the Koran numbers it among the most blessed trees. What husbandry yields a clear profit of $300, or even $200, per acre? With half a dozen acres at most, the owner might go into 'retiracy' for the rest of his life, pitying cotton and tobacco planters, and, indeed, all the anxious and painstaking industrial classes of every kind. His trees will live at least a thousand years, beyond which he can have no earthly wants; their fruit will drop unbeaten, and almost unasked—which he has only to gather."

"It has been thought," says Lord Nugent, "from the almost indestructible vitality of the olive root, after the trunk has been cut down, or even destroyed by fire, that the old trees now seen on the Mount of Olives must be shoots from the plants which were in existence 1800 years ago."

We may say of this desert as a traveller says of another, "It is true that the Sahara is a desert, but it is no more a barren unvarying wilderness than the Highlands are one continued moor. The palm trees round the wells of water form green islands, often so numerous as to be truly archipelagos, in the midst of a wide ocean of plains and mountains."

Whether there is a natural graveled or paved road, with wells for each day's journey, as Lord Lindsay describes, between the country bordering the Jordan and the Euphrates, so that we can now introduce passenger coaches, wagons for passage, mails, and specie, or a transit similar to that which has been kept up for years between Cairo and Suez, no one knows. The remarkable wells which are to be met with on this desert, or Artesian wells, now so much in vogue in many portions of our country, even in the great American Desert and in California, may be used for more than transit purposes. Successful experiments have been made to "furnish water to overflow the surface abundantly for irrigation" on the American Desert. A description of these is contained in a report to the Secretary of War, by Capt. J. Pope, of the U. S. Topographical Engineers. This is dated November, 1856, and consists of a brief synopsis of the operations. The expedition under the charge of Capt. Pope has been engaged for the past two years in testing the practicability of procuring water by means of Artesian wells on the high table lands of Texas and New Mexico, in connection with the surveys for a Pacific railroad near the 32d parallel of latitude. The latest articles of intelligence from Algeria, relate to the digging of such wells, the opening of markets for the native tribes, and the exportation of corn and other produce. Those who visited the Paris Exhibition will remember the "Algerian Trophy"—the dates from Laghouat in the distant Sahara—fruits of all zones—the specimens of urtica nivea and the crin d'afrique, the last produced from the dwarf palm, and much esteemed for the stuffing of cushions and beds. From the want of hemp during the Russian war, the French in Algeria have turned the attention of merchants and manufacturers to other vegetable fibres than the cotton. The fibres of the palm tree are infinitely superior to any thing yet discovered for the manufacture of sailcloth, rope yarn, and ships' cables. The durability of this article has been well tested. It has lately met with the approbation of the examining officers of the Woolwich Dockyard in England. The capability of a country as well situated as Algiers should not be overlooked in this age of exploration and commerce.

In the report of Commander Thos. J. Page, U. S. N., on the exploration of the La Plata, the Parana, and the Uruguay, with their tributaries, it is stated "the survey embraced an extent of river course of 3600 miles, and of actual exploration or travel by land of 4400 miles." The Government of the United States may, therefore, now equally well explore Syrian Arabia.

The date palm in Arabia thrives even where the ground is covered with salt. The cultivation of coffee can be increased to any extent. The Khat, a kind of tea plant, is already well known in Yemen; and such is the passion for it there, that it bears a very high price. It is said to promote social feelings, serenity of temper, sprightliness, and power of enduring fatigue. The Arabs of certain districts have already learned to irrigate so as to prevent the water from being dissipated in its transit. They use tunnels or subterranean canals. In Omán these cover an extent of many miles. Their height allows a man to walk upright in them. Nejd possesses the finest breeds of horses, large numbers of which were exported to India in the beginning of the present century. The introduction of the camel into our conntry is now considered of such importance that "Mr. Heap, in carrying out the project of our government, will probably make a visit into the interior of Asia Minor, in pursuance of his instructions." The camels of Nejd, one division of Arabia, are famed for their speed and beauty; for riding purposes they are unrivaled.

We should remark, that the imminent danger supposed to attend the occurrence of storms of wind in the desert—the sherky (sirocco) or *east wind*, loaded with fine sand—exists only in the tales of credulous travelers. Whatever inconveniences are endured, caravans are never buried in overwhelming sands, nor men and cattle suffocated. Snow in our climate is more than a match for sand storms.

Besides the perfumes of the interior, of poetical celebrity, the pearl banks in the Persian Gulf extend from Bahrein about 300 miles. These give employment, it is said, to nearly 30,000 men in above 3000 boats, and yield about $400,000 yearly. The pearls are nearly all bought by the Banyans, who engross still more completely the produce of the pearl fishery in the Red Sea, on the coast of the Hejáz.

The most remarkable event in the history of Arabia since the age of the Prophet, is probably that which closed the career of the Wahába, a sect of religious reformers. They threatened not only Bagdad, but Mecca, and thus provoked the hostility of the Pasha of Egypt. This occurred towards the close of the last century. Since that event, Hejáz and a part of Yemen have remained under the rule of the Pasha of Egypt.

It seems certain that the trade routes of the Arabs, in the earliest ages—in the flourishing days of Tyre and Sidon, nearly coincided with those followed in the days of the Caliphs;

when the caravans started from Bahrein for Bagdad, and thence crossed the Syrian desert to Aleppo, Damascus, or Egypt; or from Dhofár and the ports of Hadramaút they passed through Yemen on their way north. There are authentic accounts of caravans to Mecca which numbered 120,000 camels. Now-a-days, the ordinary commercial caravans rarely exceed from 500 to 1000 loaded camels. These, with guides, merchants, and followers of all kinds, on horses, asses, &c., resemble in their march a little army. These caravans are now, at times, exceedingly numerous.

The whole oasis of El-Ahsa, a fertile district of eastern Arabia, formerly called Hajar, is supposed to contain a population of 50,000. The word Ahsa is said to signify a place where water, sinking through the surface of the ground, is retained beneath. The domestic industry of El-Ahsa consists wholly in rearing camelots, and making Abas or overcoats; but the inhabitants derive large sums annually from the sale of camels and of dates; and all the trade between the coast of the Persian Gulf and the Bedouins of the Nejd, passes through this oasis. The coast of the Persian Gulf, unlike that of Syria and Palestine, has been surveyed. We can, therefore, state on good authority, that Grane (Arabic, El-Kueit) is a seaport about 85 miles south of Bussora: it is near the northern extremity of this Gulf, in the district of El-Ahsa. The bay has good anchorage, is safe and well protected by the island Felihe or Pheliche. It is about 60 miles in circuit, and has water for the largest vessels. The town is inhabited by numerous rich merchants, who possess about 800 native vessels, in which they trade to the Red Sea, and to Scinde, Gujerat, and other parts of India, whence they import grain and other goods, with which, and with coffee, they supply the interior of Arabia. The route directly across rather than that of sailing around Arabia, would create a new trade coastwise with northern Africa, and especially with Egypt. The influence of the Jewish population of the seaports has already been hinted at, as a great centre of commerce opening new and changing the present routes of transit and traffic. We regard Syrian Arabia as not at all wanting in attractions, and most especially for the great maritime powers. All are interested, because the most powerful empire in the world is that which from its geographical position possesses the greatest commercial advantages. On that account the colony which would speedily form on the Desert of Syria, would consist of an amalgamation, as well as of the enterprise, of all nations. The vast plains of the El-Hamâd or Ed-Dahna, if not the commercial centre of the world, is at least so of the eastern hemisphere. We see how easily the commercial restoration and consequent colonization of Syria and Palestine may be effected. All will concede that what is most wanted now is a colony between Russia and India, one which will as rapidly as possible unite the strength and intelligence of the world. This would be a living barrier of more value than a Sebastopol. The planting of such a colony would be friendly to all, as it would give an impetus to the commerce not only of Central but of all Asia. The Jews of Poland and Russia, and of every country, would add to the growth of such a colony. This must take place from their praiseworthy desire throughout the world to settle where commerce will improve their condition. Not only Germany, Greece, and Europe generally, but Persia, with the powers of Central Asia, would be influenced by ties of self-interest. The commerce between Caubul, Cashmere, Bokhara *via* Herat, as well as India, must take new roads to the Mediterranean Sea. The gold of Australia, Sumatra, and what may be discovered in Arabia and other portions of the East, will soon demand another channel to Europe.

Science and commerce are rapidly advancing in the East, and this partly by the late war. This is shown by the railroads in contemplation, such as that from Vienna to Constantinople, via Belgrade, now authorized by the Sultan's government—by that from France, *via* Lake of Geneva, Turin, Milan, to the Adriatic Sea—the canal to be constructed connecting the river Danube with the Black Sea—the great ship canal of the Isthmus of Suez—the present India route through Egypt connecting Alexandria with Suez by railroad—the railroads and plans not yet completed of "The Euphrates Valley Railway Company," connecting the ancient port of Seleucia with Aleppo—also that from the ancient seaport Joppa, now Jaffa, to Jerusalem, and thence to Damascus. The plans of "The Euphrates V. R. R. Co." avoid entirely the Syrian Desert. Their lines are mostly to the east of the Euphrates and west of the Tigris possibly owing to the immediate necessities arising from the political situation of Herat and the war with Persia.

Every American statesman as well as merchant should study the trade of the East, now that telegraphs are preparing to unite Ceylon and Calcutta with Cuba and New Orleans—when Europe is proposing so many routes to increase the trade in the Levant by opening Asia as well as Africa to commerce. The lines of proposed railway connecting Trieste, Belgrade, and Hungary with Salonica, Munich with Vienna, the Danube with the Grecian Archipelago,—are but indications of what may take place.

We look upon the Persian Gulf and the river Tigris as well adapted to steamers of the American pattern; because not only "the trade of the Persian Gulf with India is three to one that of the Red Sea, but it is obvious that the Persian Gulf presents such facilities for steam navigation, and can be navigated by steamers of such small dimensions." Besides "the river Tigris is navigable at all times of the year between Korna and Bagdad," for steamboats drawing more water than can, at certain seasons, possibly float on the Euphrates.

If we unite the only good natural harbors on the Syrian coast of the Mediterranean Sea and Persian Gulf by a line, it passes entirely to the west of the river Euphrates. This line extended and representing a trunk railroad, has important and extraordinary relations with more than one country. A railroad has been projected as straight as the country, and the vast but well-adapted desert plains will admit, between the port of Alexandretta on the Mediterranean Sea and that of Grane on the Persian Gulf. The most correct maps exhibit how such a trunk road, as it were, binds together two great lines, viz.—one drawn from London to Sidney, and the other from London to Bombay. As the trade of Syria, on the Mediterranean Sea, is chiefly confined to Alexandretta, Tripoli, and Beyrout, especially the last, various branch roads have been proposed. It has been thought best, however, first to unite Beyrout, by the pass in Lebanon, near Sidon, with Damascus. This connects the two most populous cities of the country, and at the same time passes through and near the most fertile sections of Syria and Palestine. In order to gain a point nearer a natural center for the caravan trade of the Desert, this branch should be extended to Tadmor (Palmyra). A branch from Tripoli to Tadmor would certainly be the shortest. The nature of the country, however, may not admit of its construction in any way better than a zigzag line. That proposed from Seleucia to Aleppo is too far to the north for our wants. On reaching a point to the east of Tadmor by the Beyrout branch, as suggested, a portion of the trunk railway could most speedily be commenced southerly to Grane, which connects by the Persian Gulf with the waters of the Indus, &c. That portion of the trunk railway to the north of Tadmor, towards Alexandretta, and an easterly branch towards Bagdad and Persia, could be undertaken more slowly if thought advisable.

The Euphrates in this plan is principally used to irrigate the desert sections, and furnish the road and settlements with water. A junction, finally, of the Euphrates with Tadmor by a canal of navigation and irrigation, as another "Baree Doab" in the Punjaub, India, will supply all that possibly may be required, or that the springs of water which exist there will not be able to supply in the future. The increased commerce and population of the first sections would, by such a canal, possibly anticipate and sufficiently prepare the country of the southern section of the Euphrates, and bordering the Shat-el-Arab, for the more speedy and substantial construction of the railway to Grane. The serious difficulty to be overcome in all the plans yet suggested, is the overflowing, and consequent unhealthy condition, of the country near and below the junction of the rivers Tigris and Euphrates.

This project is looked upon as self-supporting from its local trade. In its beginning, and especially its desert section, it connects and increases the caravan commerce of Central Asia, at a better point than has yet been proposed. The transit to India, from the Mediterranean Sea, is equally affected by the same means. The carrying out of the plans would expedite the *complete* establishment of the principle of toleration and religious freedom, as set forth in the recent concessions of the Sublime Porte.

The restoration of a desert has not been connected with any plan as far as known, although all have admitted that there is a great want of water in certain places, not excepting even "that great river."

It is thought that there is enough to do; that Anglo-American enterprise would most speedily form a politico-commercial union of great advantage to both nations, especially in developing the dormant resources of that portion of the East. This plan would contribute its share to ameliorate the condition of vast populations, and finally give them even a higher grade of civilization than we enjoy.

The air lines from London to Sydney or Bombay, intersect some of the most prominent commercial emporiums of Europe, Asia, the East Indies, and Australia. Among others should be mentioned Strasbourg, Trieste, Constantinople, and Batavia. Besides these lines, others equally striking and interesting might be drawn. Baron Von Haxthausen's work on Transcaucasia, shows, in the preface, lines not generally known to the world. Among other ideas, we should not neglect to mention the importance of the irrigation of the desert with reference, to the ravages of the locust, to the avoiding to so large an extent the difficulties of keeping in repair the embankments of the river Euphrates, and the annoyances arising from some Arab tribes. By the cultivation of trees, already referred to, the rains would most probably be restored, and the desert speedily made to contribute to the support of a great trunk railroad. The late discoveries in the manufacture of iron; the great speed attainable by the enlarged locomotive; the recent improvements in submarine engineering by "the nautilus," and its adaptation to the construction of harbors, prove that individual, and even national interest is fast merging into that of all mankind. The shortest line from the Mediterranean Sea to the Persian Gulf would connect Joppa and Grane. The true complement of the Isthmus of Suez Canal is this southern line of railroad. The increasing trade, after the construction of either of these projects, would render the other indispensable. A southern direct line of railway would have to depend on artesian wells for water, at least for that portion of the Syrian desert where it is impossible to use the waters of the Jordan and Euphrates. The depression of the valley of the Jordan might possibly be avoided by running to the south of the Dead Sea; but here, judging from our want of knowledge, there is need of exploration. Until further investigation on the advantages of Wady Sirhan, the disputed levels of the Syrian desert, and other points briefly set forth in "The Report of the Committee on resuming the U. S. Expedition to the Jordan and Dead Sea," recently published in the "Bulletin of the American Geographical and Statistical Society," we cannot speak confidently of the comparative merits of any plans. A general hydrographic reconnoissance, or the survey of the coast of Syria and Palestine, especially of that portion near and to the south of Jaffa, is much wanted. What the present improvements in submarine engineering could effect at any point on the coast bordering the desert section of Palestine, is not known. All the maritime powers, not excepting ourselves, are interested in a speedy survey of this portion of the Levant.

Our increasing trade with India alone, is appreciated by the following foreign-news item: "When the mails left Calcutta, October 8th, 1856, there were lying in the Hoogly about 140,000 tons of shipping, a large part of it American." The single article of India rubber, which formerly was only obtained from South America, is now more cheaply imported from the East Indies. The demand for it is constantly increasing. This is but one fact with reference to our trade in the East.

The Boston and Salem merchants are largely concerned in the East India trade, especially with Sumatra and other great islands in that part of the world, as is seen in the memorial presented to Congress since the beginning of the year, which arose from the pretended monopoly of the Indian Archipelago, by Holland. We quote from this, and an able Report presented at the first session of the present Congress. "The Indian Archipelago, including the inland seas pertaining thereto, is equal in extent to the surface of the United States and territories, and contains a population of about 27,000,000 souls. The largest islands are Borneo, New Guinea, Sumatra, Java, &c. That the attention of the commercial world has long been drawn to the importance of opening new fields of trade in the extensive regions of the East; and especially in the group of islands known as those of the East Indian Archipelago. Your committee regard it as highly important that diplomatic and consular agents should be sent to one or more points in the Archipelago; that treaties should be made with the native princes, laying the basis for lasting friendship and extended commerce, and providing against the creation of any future monopolies, or the territorial extension of any of those existing." The United States are inquiring into the expediency of sending a commissioner to the islands of the East Indian Archipelago, with powers to investigate the claims of sovereignty which the government of the Netherlands asserts to possess over most of the Islands, and of forming treaties with such independent states and tribes, as may be found thereon of sufficient power and importance to render such treaties necessary. We have special advantages for carrying on trade with the Indian Archipelago from the port of San Francisco, and with Central Asia and India by the Mediterranean Sea, from our Atlantic ports, provided Syrian Arabia was open to commerce. The internal and external evidences of great changes in China and Central Asia, are weighty arguments in favor of exploration.

It is only by railroads on the Syrian Desert, that Great Britain, France, the Jews as a people, the United States, the Mohammedans, including Arabs and others, can be commercially united. Either railway, the shortest being about 850 miles, map measurement, would traverse the entire length of the plain of the El-Hamâd or Ed-Dahna, the Arabia Deserta of the old geographers, and Syrian Desert of others. It would almost seem that it was for this that God created the vast plains of the El-Hamâd, as their formation is most remarkably adapted for this purpose. Neither hills, mountains, nor valleys are found on the great plain as far as it is known. Besides the use which could be made of the plain of Aleppo, and the flat country and hard soil near the Euphrates, there is said to be "a midway ridge" which might answer for a natural water-shed or for a common road. This is crossed by the great road 100 feet wide, now said to be as well paved as any street in Paris or London, and with wells for each day's journey. This paved road is justly called the greatest work of that astonishing people, the old Romans. For useful purposes these are matters of exploration.

Volunteer individual effort can yet do much, as it has already done in the expedition to the river Jordan and the Dead Sea. The geological reconnoissance of the Lebanon mountains by Henry J. Anderson, M. D., LL. D., has received its well-merited praise from both sides of the Atlantic. What influence any one individual can exert to procure such information as is wanted, in order more speedily to bring about its attendant blessing, is best known to themselves. On this Desert, irrigation is alone wanted for a successful cultivation of the soil throughout the year. This is shown after rains, by the flower-bearing bushes and good pasture. To supply this deficiency it is thought possible to turn the Euphrates and the Jordan into the Desert. The "narrow and wonderful ravines," of about 100 feet in depth, the old beds of the Euphrates, the gigantic ancient canals wanting so little repair, are all adapted to this purpose.

The proposed magnificent harbors of Alexandretta and Grane, not only rival the finest in the world, but are most advantageously situated. The old inland basins at Seleucia, forty-seven acres in extent, "the Euphrates Valley Railway Company" expect to put in good order for the railway to Aleppo. The cost of this and another artificial harbor near Jaffa, cannot be told until the proper surveys and estimates have been made. The junction of the southern line of railroad by a coastwise branch, or one through the valley of the Jordan or the Haouran, so as to unite with the road at Beyrout, Damascus, or even with Egypt, it is only necessary to mention.

The connecting sea-routes through the Mediterranean Sea, would bind together many nations. A canal piercing the

Isthmus of Corinth six miles, would extend commerce through Greece and her archipelago to Austria and all Germany, also over northern Italy to France and Great Britain. Either of the Syrian Desert trunk railroads would become as it were a new Dardanelles and Bosphorus, not to a Black Sea, but to an Indian Ocean and the great Pacific. International companies may yet open those roads so that all nations may be equally interested, and their vessels of commerce act as a mutual check the one upon the other. In this way it is possible that vessels of war may finally lose their importance.

If India alone, with a population little less than 200,000,000, advancing in productive industry every year, requires a railway of over 1,000 miles in length so zigzag in its course as to touch at Shuster for the best opium, or at Bagdad to politically influence Persia, it will be built, and that possibly by the Euphrates Valley Railway Company. For they say, "We are far from accepting the Ja'ber Castle line as the final solution of the great problem—the shortest route to India. We accept it as an installment only, confidently looking forward to the day when the company which now proposes the first step in the right road, will carry out the extension of their line, and connect the Mediterranean and the Persian Gulf by an iron road." The cost of building or taking a Sebastopol, it is unnecessary to ask. The commercial man, as well as the statesman, should study the influence of such a road on the true development of that country, especially Syrian Arabia. It is for this we are in want of better maps, only to be obtained by exploration.

The shortest possible routes to India, China, and Australia, are now not only attracting the statesman, merchant, capitalist, but even the philanthropist; because what increases commerce benefits all. The Syrian Desert is therefore the most important of the great thoroughfares by sea and land, being the link to unite and civilize all mankind by commerce. A desirable result might be obtained could such roads as are proposed, not only be constructed by the combined skill, and exemplify the peculiarities of taste, durability, and speed, of French, English, and American engineers, but the exploration be primarily conducted under their various national but united talent. If our government took the lead in this matter, it would be followed by others, as has been done both in the late Japan Expedition and in deep-sea soundings across the Atlantic Ocean.

In a memoir, dated London, January, 1857, and dedicated to the Earl of Clarendon, by W. P. Andrew, F. R. G. S., it is stated that "the route to Australia by way of Southampton, Alexandria, and Suez, is practically quicker by ten days than by way of Panama. It is a common mistake that the road viâ the Isthmus of Panama is the shortest from London to Sidney. The two routes stand in the relation of 8,400 geographical miles viâ the Euphrates, and of 9,900 geographical miles viâ the Isthmus of Panama, or 1,500 geographical miles in favor of the Euphrates route."

To facilitate intercourse, and relieve the necessities of Christians, Jews, and Mohammedans in the East—to spread civilization where it has been entirely neglected and is most needed, viz., among the Arabs, we know of no better instrumentality. For the Arab may be said to be especially neglected; when missionaries are exploring the interior of Africa, and being settled even among the Affghans. As either road would most permanently and intimately unite all nations and creeds, the popularity of the enterprise could only be measured by its influence in annihilating the deplorable prejudices existing among all religious sects, and in no place exercising more influence than in the Eastern world.

An interesting paper, principally on the physical features of the Holy Land and Syria, was read during the past season before "The American Geographical and Statistical Society," by the Rev. M. J. Raphall, Dr. Ph. The learned rabbi stated that the idea of a road through the Syrian Desert was not new; that he claimed no originality, and if he wanted to go back to its first publication he would quote the Prophet Isaiah. He gave the following translation of his Hebrew quotation—"Behold, I bring you something new, and even now it shall spring forth. Will you not recognize it? I will cause a road to be made through the wilderness, and rivers to flow through the desert." Most probably before, but certainly as early as 1535, we meet with this singular English translation of this sacred writer (Isaiah, lxi. 4), by Myles Coverdale—"They shal buylde the long rough wildernes, and set up the olde deserte. They shal repayre the waist places and soch as haue bene uoyde thorow out many generacions." It is a little remarkable that the commercial restoration and consequent colonization of Syria, can be brought about by a railroad; that this would introduce a general system of fertilizing the sands of the desert by irrigation, render indispensable the Isthmus of Suez Canal; that this canal and the Syrian-desert railroads would eventually "turn the rivers into the desert" (Psalms, cvii. verses 33, 36, 37), "dry up the Euphrates" (Revelations, xvi. 12), "destroy the tongue of the Egyptian Sea," by means of the barrage and the proposed canal of alimentation (Isaiah xi. 15), "heal the waters of the Dead Sea" (Ezekiel, xlvii. 10, 11). These portions of Scripture, so simply explained, are, with a road, prophetical (Isaiah, xlviii. 19). The sword and the spear of the Arab are, it seems, to be used for the purposes of agriculture (Isaiah, ii. 4). It is in this Desert that they are in common use, but more for the destruction than the support of our fellow-creatures. Could they be used to turn the course of the irrigating rivulets, civilization would soon commence among the wildest people, leading, ultimately, to the reign of universal peace.

It has not been our intention to go into any minutiæ, or even to cover the ground of our views on the subject of the commercial importance of Syrian Arabia. We desire to attract attention by merely hinting at the one-sided views so prevalent in each hemisphere, by losing sight of the central position of Syrian Arabia, in that which in size is more than double our own, and in its population vastly superior. We think it important to make of easy access for the invalid, that part of our globe which is thought to possess the finest, as well as the most peculiar climate—one that will not only give durability to railroads, but is admirably adapted for the great staples of commerce. We have hinted at many articles,—among others, of a substitute for the 40,000,000 pounds of tea which we import from China, of the profit of the cultivation of the olive, and the many uses of the palm. We have neglected to speak of other trees, as the fig, or mulberry ; the last-mentioned now cultivated in some places from the base to the top of Mount Lebanon. The leaves are used to fatten sheep, as well as for silk worms. We might have referred to the coal and iron, as well as bitumen. Major-General Chesney thinks the bitumen can be furnished for fuel at a price not to exceed six cents per 112 lbs., even at Ja'ber Castle on the Euphrates.

We have in part described the peculiar and extraordinary position and advantages of the Jewish nation, of their influence upon, and the trade they can open up, even with the Arabs ; that the Arabs of some portions of their country form an intermediate class between vagrant tribes and peasants ; that they are settled as petty merchants in a continued line of small towns, and at present conduct caravans through this desert ; that they have ingenious methods of irrigation.

We might have spoken of the Armenians. Their industrious habits cause them to be preferred as tenants by the Mahommedan landlord, both in Turkey and Persia. Russia has shown her appreciation of this people when, in her wars with Persia and Turkey, she introduced many thousand families into Georgia. There is a striking uniformity in their character in all parts of the world, at least in Turkey, Persia, Russia, and India. They are most keen and indefatigable traders. The limits of their commercial enterprise in the East are Tartary and China. An Armenian was the first to discover the present route via Trebizond and Tebriz, for that commerce which formerly passed through Bushire and Bagdad. Of what benefit such a people would be in developing the commerce of Syrian Arabia, is easily inferred.

The proposed lines of road are located mostly on caravan routes. This would begin a new trade from and to all quarters, exemplified by crossing, rather than doubling, the whole of Arabia, and thus acting commercially on northern Africa.

We like these views of a late article in Tait's Magazine, on the Euphrates Valley Railway, that "the friends of this scheme are now opening out a country equally fertile but much larger than Egypt itself. As for India, it has a trade that will afford two roads in or out; however the Calcutta, Ceylon, and Madras trade may run, the Indus business will flow into the Euphratean channel. As to grain, with means of transport Mesopotamia would pour incalculable supplies, at prices far below those for the same article in the Black Sea. Many millions of inhabitants crowded the banks of the Euphrates in ancient days. Their power was felt over all western Asia and northern Africa. The now deserted plains were fields and gardens. The soil teemed with vegetation. The fruits of temperate and tropical climes grew there in luscious abundance. The arid sands need only again to be irrigated by the abounding waters to become joyous with corn, wine, and oil." The same writer says of three great lines of railway meeting at the termini in London, "They take widely divergent courses, and neither of them could alone have accommodated the intermediate traffic; this, he thinks, is an analogous case to the Indian business, which can well support two or three routes from end to end."

A complete substitute for the river Euphrates on a ridge supposed to be a natural watershed, using the depressions on the adjoining desert reservoirs or pools for irrigation, turning the rivers for that purpose into the narrow but deep ravines on the north, using the existing canals on the south, making immediate use of the road which is supposed to exist, employing the Arabs with their camels and horses at once: this is one outline of our views. The other or southern line may, after a hydrographic reconnoissance, be found not only the shortest, but as furnishing less difficulties than have been hinted at.

To witness the rising of the sun on the Persian Gulf, the awe-striking but placid lake which marks a mysterious cemetery, the "beautiful for situation" from the east, of the mountains of Jerusalem, and the sun's setting rays falling gently over the Mediterranean,—as has been ably described, may, with a speed of sixty miles the hour, yet be made to occupy but one day, and that not far distant.

Were it proper, we could dwell on the lengthened life promised by the known effects of such an atmosphere as covers the desert mountains near Ma'an—of the best development of the physique, which exists there ; but the influence and the fragrance of this atmosphere arise from a medical botany unfortunately as yet unknown.

The labors of a Wallin, and Burton, and of the U. S. Expedition to the Jordan and Dead Sea, had but few objects of science in view. The resuming of this last expedition will combine many. It may attempt to make commercial treaties with those tribes which frequent this portion of Arabia. The levels of the plains adjoining the Dead Sea; the field of antiquarian research in the ruins of known but unvisited cities, paved roads, wells, ravines; the peculiar botany of the country,—these and other matters have been described in another paper. Knowledge, which is power, is wanted of the locality as connected with this home of the horse and the camel, and also of its mineral wealth. We have hinted at the comparison of the proposed expedition with what has been done by the viceroy of Egypt, and other foreign powers; with the extent and distance of those undertaken by the United States to Japan, and, among others, that of the vast interior of South America; and more especially of the want of a hydrographic reconnoisance of a portion of the coast of Palestine bordering the desert. The benefits of such expeditions are not for commerce alone. They not only ameliorate the conditions of all races, and lessen the prejudices of religious sects, but they are the true field on which our navy has already gained some laurels. A reference to the standard maps of Stieler and Berghaus, Zimmerman and Ritter, Chesney, Johnston, and others, shows how little is known and what is wanted. It is unnecessary to examine the reports of the various geographical societies, to be convinced that we know but little. Every new traveler proves it. This becomes most important, as the affairs of the East compel the construction of a great road, which, as Americans, we ought at least to turn to some profit.

An expedition of any one nation to explore Syrian Arabia will hardly have an opportunity to tread this Desert before it is followed by that of another, unless it be undertaken by the maritime nations as proposed. The question is, who shall and ought to take the lead?

THE MEMORIAL.

TO THE HONORABLE THE SECRETARY OF THE NAVY OF THE UNITED STATES OF AMERICA.

The Memorial of the American Geographical and Statistical Society, respectfully showeth:

That the attention of your Memorialists has been attracted to the interesting region between the Jordan and the Euphrates, and southward through the plain of El-Hamâd, a country formerly renowned and flourishing, but now, and during many centuries, one of the least known in the Eastern Hemisphere.

That in the year 1847, the admiration of foreign nations was called forth by the expedition the United States sent out to explore the Dead Sea, in the interests of science. Lieut. W. F. Lynch, U. S. N., the officer in command, acquitted himself with great ability to the full extent of his instructions, which, however, as he regrets, did not authorize him to carry his researches beyond the Dead Sea.

Your Memorialists have reason to believe that the resuming of this expedition, by order and under the auspices of the U. S. Navy Department, might probably lead to important discoveries in geography, geology, and medical botany. Your Memorialists even entertain the expectation that such an expedition is likely to be rewarded by the finding of an ancient city—equal to Petra—with its unrifled monuments the existence of which is lately become known, though no European or American as yet has visited the ruins.

That at this particular time the Ottoman government is engaged in establishing throughout its dominions a system of civil and religious equality, offensive to the fanaticism of Mahometans, but conducive to the best interests of humanity. That in the carrying out of this praiseworthy but arduous measure, the government of the Sultan would be encouraged and strengthened by the moral support of any great power other than those concerned in the late Congress of Paris. For they are viewed by the Mahometans with distrust, and their support carries with it the appearance of coercion. Whereas moral support from the United States—a power great as the greatest, but perfectly disinterested except inasmuch as this republic is the only assertor and protector of religious equality—would be justly and highly appreciated by the populations as well as by the government of the Ottoman empire; so that, under Providence, it may perhaps become the means of enabling American enterprise to recall into life the long dormant, but still great, capabilities of Syrian Arabia, introducing to those countries the blessings of civilization, and opening to the United States and to the world new and highly valuable lines of commerce.

That in view of results so important, the American Geographical and Statistical Society would deem it a duty to associate itself with the conducting of an expedition which in point of distance and difficulty compares favorably with others sent out by the United States, and at the same time will be found second to none in advancing the glory of this country and the welfare of mankind.

Your Memorialists, therefore, respectfully suggest the necessity of resuming the Dead Sea expedition, under instructions and with powers adapted to the realizing of the expectations in this memorial set forth.

Approved by the American Geographical and Statistical Society, May, 1856.

ELBERT H. CHAMPLIN, M. D.
ARCHIBALD RUSSELL.
MORRIS J. RAPHALL, Ph. D.
HENRY V. POOR.
JOSEPH P. THOMPSON, D. D.
MELANCTON SMITH, Commander, U. S. N.
HENRY J. ANDERSON, M. D., LL. D.
SIDNEY MASON.

Committee on Syrian Exploration.

www.ingramcontent.com/pod-product-compliance
Lightning Source LLC
LaVergne TN
LVHW011136110826
845150LV00008B/2370
* 9 7 8 1 4 1 8 1 9 3 7 7 5 *